THE PATCH

THE PATCH

Justina Chen Headley

Illustrated by **Mitch Vane**

Charlesbridge

On the day Becca turned five, she pirouetted into the doctor's office. In the waiting room she took out paper and drew triangles and circles and squares. Heart-shaped tulips. And squiggly worms. She spelled her name: B-E-C-C-A. And then her dog's name: F-I-G-A-R-O. She counted to seventy-seven. And when Becca got her shots, she didn't cry more than three tears. Maybe four . . .

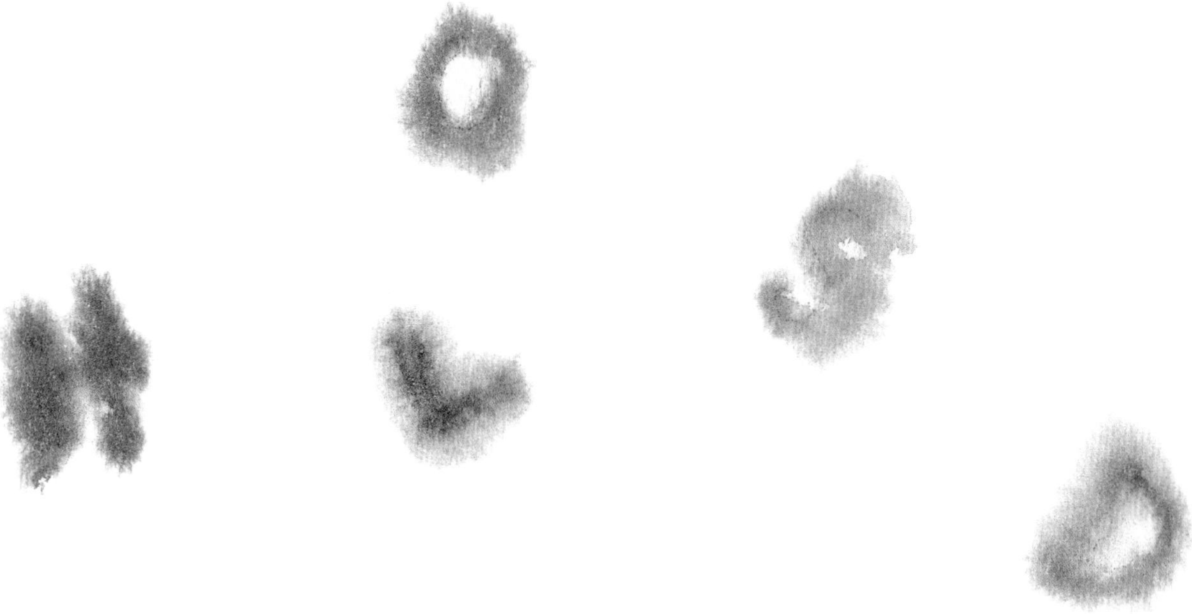

O

H L S

D

. . . until she stood in front of the eye
chart and her left eye read fuzz balls
instead of letters.

The doctor told Becca, "You get to wear
glasses to help you see better and an eye
patch to make your left eye stronger."

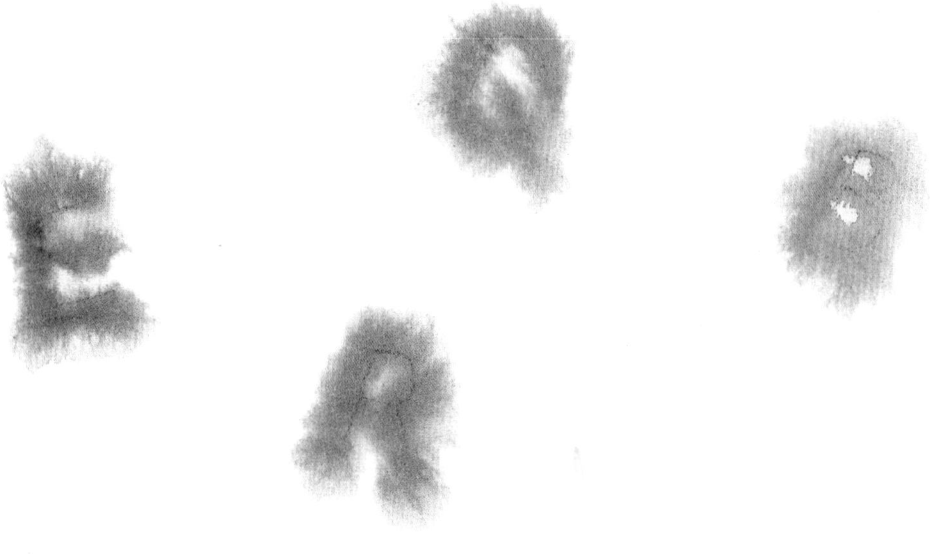

Q B

E

R

"Ballerinas don't wear glasses," Becca cried.
"And they especially do NOT wear patches!"
"Ballerinas who want to see the stage
when they dance do," said her mother.
And that was that.

Still, Becca shook her head at the glittery gold eyeglasses. She frowned at the flamingo pink frames. She even turned her back on the ruby red ones. Finally, Becca decided purple glasses and a pink patch might be an acceptable fashion statement for a prima ballerina.

But the next morning, Becca wouldn't budge out of bed.

"Everyone is going to think I look stupid," bawled Becca.

"Lots of kids your age wear glasses," her mother replied. "Like your friend Kusiima."

"But he doesn't have to wear a patch," said Becca.

Her bedroom door cracked open, and her big brother, Brian, whispered, "You can borrow my pirate costume. But just this once."

Before her brother could change his mind, Becca threw off her blanket, rushed into his bedroom, and grabbed his all-time favorite costume. She tied on the red cloak and buttoned up the poofy purple pants. Then she put on her glasses and rescued her pink patch from under Figaro's bed.

"I am Becca the Ballerina Pirate, who dances across the seven seas," bellowed Becca. "And I command you to dance the jig with me."

Brian stared at her. "Are you kidding?"

Becca the Ballerina Pirate, who danced across the seven seas, twirled into her classroom.

"Cute glasses, but why are you wearing a patch?" asked her very best friend, Sophia Lou.

"Because, matey, I'm in search of a secret treasure," Becca the Ballerina Pirate answered. She hollered over to her other friends who took ballet with her. "Are you all with me?"

"Aye aye, cap'n," saluted Sophia Lou, Kusiima, and Ellie.

Becca the Ballerina Pirate and her pirate pals jetéd over 20-foot wild waves. They pliéd on the heads of five ferocious crocodiles that were guarding the treasure chest. Gracefully, each balancing on one foot, they snatched up the secret treasures. Then Becca and her pirate crew sailed off to circle time.

During circle time, Sophia Lou asked again, "Why are you wearing a patch?"

"Because I am Becca the Private Eye, who can find anything," explained Becca.

"Even my lost sweater?" Sophia Lou wanted to know.

Becca the Private Eye burrowed into the lost-and-found box. She rummaged through a pile of books. She crawled around the Craft Corner . . . and snapped up Sophia Lou's sweater from under a stack of popsicle sticks.

"Oooooh!" the class exclaimed, very impressed.

At recess, Sophia Lou asked, "Why are you really wearing a patch?"

"Because I am Becca the One-Eyed Monster!" shouted Becca.

Becca the One-Eyed Monster howled.
She growled. And she chased the boys halfway
around the playground until Miss Kearney
told her that monsters—no matter how many
eyes they had—weren't welcome at school.

By the end of the day, the entire class demanded patches of their own.

Miss Kearney asked Becca, "Can you tell the class why you're really wearing eyeglasses and a patch?"

"Because I have a lazy eye," Becca said importantly.

"No fair!" grumbled Kusiima.

A few weeks later, Sophia Lou returned from a skiing trip with a cast on her arm.

"Why are you wearing a cast?" asked Becca during recess.

"Because I am Sophia Lou the Superhero, who can freeze anything with just one wave of my elbow," she answered.

"That's funny. So can I," said Becca, waving her elbow at the playground.

And the two superhero best friends ran off to wave their elbows at everything.

Author's Note

Amblyopia [am-blee-OH-pee-ah], also called lazy eye, is a loss of vision in an eye due to the lack of its use in early childhood. Around four out of every 100 children under the age of six suffer from amblyopia.

Wearing an eye patch is one way to treat amblyopia. The patch covers up the stronger eye so that a child has to use the weaker eye to see. Just as exercising can make a person's muscles grow larger, putting a patch over the stronger eye can strengthen the weaker eye. Sometimes, in addition to wearing a patch, a child may also need to wear glasses, do eye exercises, or use eyedrops.

Pediatricians screen children for amblyopia at birth and continue screening throughout preschool years. Eye doctors recommend that children have a complete eye examination by the time they are three years old, particularly if there is a family history of amblyopia.

For Sofia, who does everything with panache
—J. C. H.

To my darling Jessica. Thank you Natalie & the C.S.P.S. preps
—M. V.

Many thanks to my wonderful editor, Randi Rivers, who made my dreams come true.
Also, thanks to Dr. Karen Preston and Dr. Bob Glaze
for their insight into amblyopia—and for being amazing eye doctors.

Text copyright © 2006 by Justina Chen Headley
Illustrations copyright © 2006 by Mitch Vane
All rights reserved, including the right of reproduction in whole or in part in any form. Charlesbridge and colophon are registered trademarks of Charlesbridge Publishing, Inc.

Published by Charlesbridge
85 Main Street
Watertown, MA 02472
(617) 926-0329
www.charlesbridge.com

Illustrations done in watercolor and dip pen and India ink on Arches watercolor paper
Text type set in Obelisk
Color separated by Chroma Graphics, Singapore
Printed and bound by Imago, Thailand
Production supervision by Brian G. Walker
Designed by Diane M. Earley

Library of Congress Cataloging-in-Publication Data
Headley, Justina Chen, 1968–
The patch / Justina Chen Headley ; illustrated by Mitch Vane.
p. cm.
Summary: At first upset about having to wear glasses and an eye patch to correct her lazy eye, five-year-old Becca soon discovers that her new accessories allow her to take on such roles as a ballerina-pirate and a private eye.
ISBN-13: 978-1-58089-049-6; ISBN-10: 1-58089-049-0 (reinforced for library use
[1. Amblyopia—Fiction. 2. Self-acceptance—Fiction. 3. Eyeglasses—Fiction. 4. Schools—Fiction.] I. Vane, Mitch, ill. II. Title.
PZ7.H3424   Pat 2006
[E]—dc22   2005006017

Printed in Thailand
(hc) 10 9 8 7 6 5 4 3 2 1